The Firestorm

The Firestorm

poems

Zach Savich

Winner of the 2010 Cleveland State University
Poetry Center Open Competition

Cleveland State University Poetry Center
Cleveland, Ohio

ISBN 978-1-880834-95-4

First edition

5   4   3   2   1

This book is published by
Cleveland State University Poetry Center,
2121 Euclid Avenue, Cleveland, Ohio 44115-2214.
www.csuohio.edu/poetrycenter and is distributed by
SPD /Small Press Distribution, Inc. www.spdbooks.org

Cover image: [... Description of a New Machine for enabling
Persons to escape from the Windows of Houses on Fire.] The Penn-
sylvania magazine, Philadelphia, 1775; Courtesy of the John Carter
Brown Library at Brown University. Cover design by Amy Freels.

The Firestorm was designed and typeset by Amy Freels in Dante
with Vintage Typewriter display.

LIBRARY OF CONGRESS CATALOGING-IN-PUBLICATION DATA
Savich, Zach.
The firestorm : poems / Zach Savich.—1st ed.
    p. cm.—(New poetry)
"Winner of the 2010 Cleveland State University Poetry Center
Open Competition."
ISBN 978-1-880834-95-4 (acid-free paper)
I. Title. II. Series.

PS3619.A858F57 2011

811'.6—DC22

2010052621

Acknowledgments

I'm grateful to the journals that first published this book's poems: *Anti-*, *Blue Mesa Review*, *Colorado Review*, *Eoagh*, *H_NGM_N*, *Jellyfish*, *Mare Nostrum*, *Now Culture*, *The Offending Adam*, *Seneca Review*, and *The Umbrella Factory*. Omnidawn published some of these poems in a chapbook, *The Man Who Lost His Head*.

Thank you, also, to the University of Massachusetts Amherst, the Cleveland State University Poetry Center, Dan Beachy-Quick, Dara Wier, Belchertown Poets, and, for every day, Hilary Plum.

for Kathy and John Savich

Contents

The Firestorm

I am content, necessarily, but not to the point of clapping my hands.

SAMUEL BECKETT

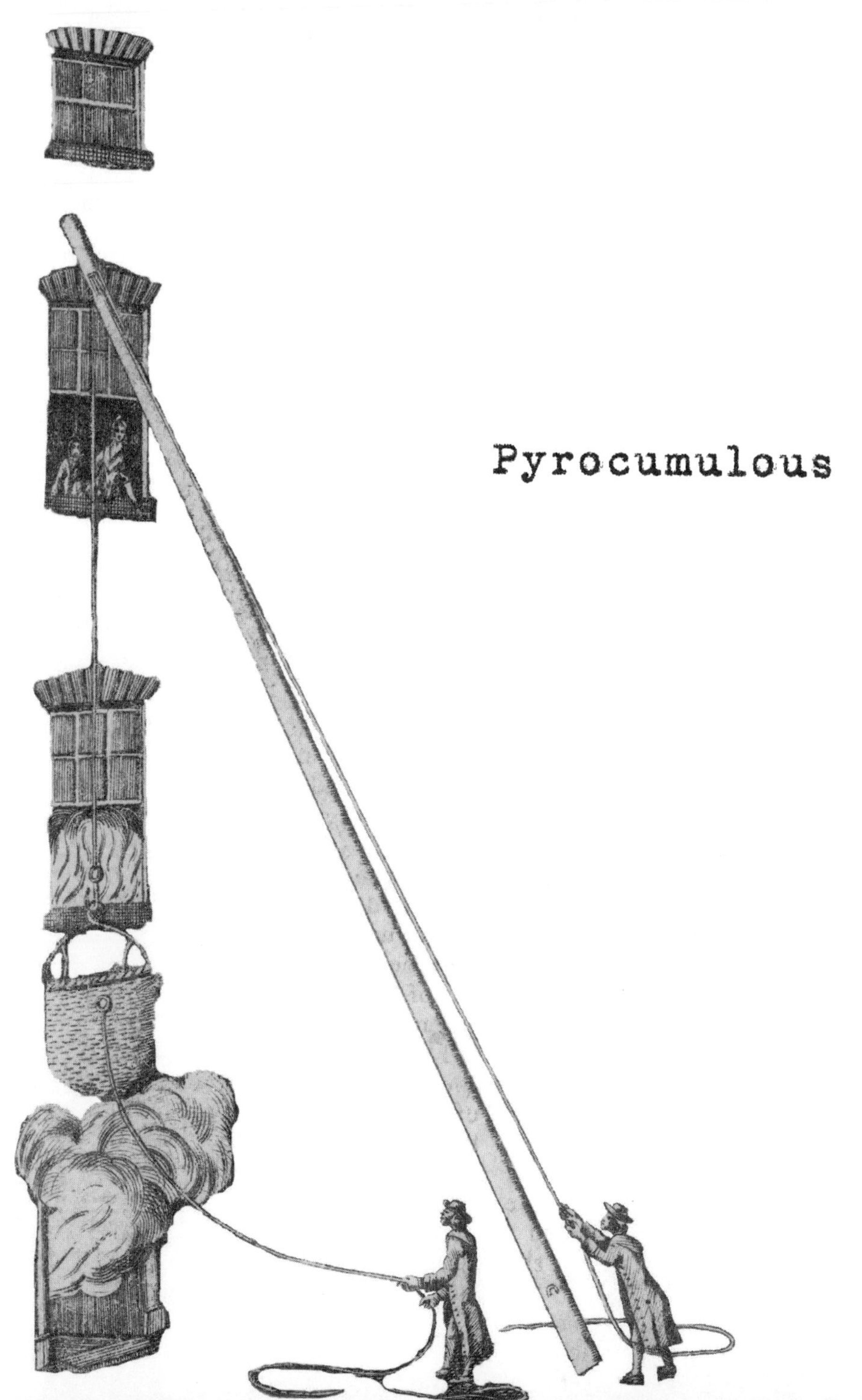
Pyrocumulous

Pyrocumulous: the firestorm constructs its own weather, around
as the leaves resembled from a hollowed apple, the peel,
a railstorm, pondstorm, constructing, there cannot be
another beginning only insistence that this is of the first instance continuing *(To apple,*
meaning to pick apples or to quarter something
as one would an apple or [appellation]
to name), a memoir of the higher frequencies, so the demand is less
expression of a soul than to locate where it is left,
fabric scrap on limb—is this it?—or it is a signaling of—*this way*—

But here is how it appears to one dying—but what if
we've been wrong about it all, and may act as every day's an armistice,
put out, like a dish of withering plums
with the sense many must have of breathing not only forever inward, granular,
gradually building only a vantage from which one
may witness where she has been. They say in every country she is
from the country, formerly a coast struck at angles to locate, eyes
as a runaway truck's ruts, smoothed to a sandy,
now lifting, now spritzing with rye. I am whatever is between hat,
glasses, and beard, hitting a note toward you from varied haggard positions—

whatever it is to *be known*—

To act forever comprehending how little this was

(an *I had a feeling*) (cursive of vein)

forever departing in the instance continuing for hills

or a dimness making hues we can manage

where one bends to the hummingbird-processed water

one then exists no more than. Numbness

literaler than pain, foregrounding feeling at the edges, strange

fidelities: two tomatoes on the table were a bulbous bird,

his story beginning: *Therefore by the end you will understand*

why my present style is so brazen—so bland—

I feel I am wearing a hat but am not. Can't even tell
if I'm sad or sick. Shared a yawn with a bus
stranger. All we've ever done is variously revise
Leaves of Grass. To leave then at the height of one's—
to leave off—sun stranded across the sky like a piano two men carry
uptown—

A Children's Story:

The village woke and every word was hell—

Hell hell hell hell hell

And every word they wrote was hell.
And numbers, too.
And the sound little birds made, animating the copper oxen bells.
And when you said your name, hell sashayed from you—

And yet

Only to be initial to another. I live a chip off the block from
Paradise Road. Paralyze?

Find the mortal world enough. But where have you been—
stayed out all night—like the milk you warned me about—

But then it's cold enough you don't mind the light.
Makes the blue look white. Makes me look

surprisingly easy—that's one kind of beautiful. Another is
I've counted the eggs.

I've counted

In bed like fishing flies in their case
choice evaporated winter apples printed on the antique scrap

And days all was riding on a pun, days of disinheritance we welcomed
like an estate sale of blades, day dreary enough you could smile

at anyone

If Love exists why remember

It is not betrayal
if you stoop to a tooth
near curb
handkerchief it

and we never meet

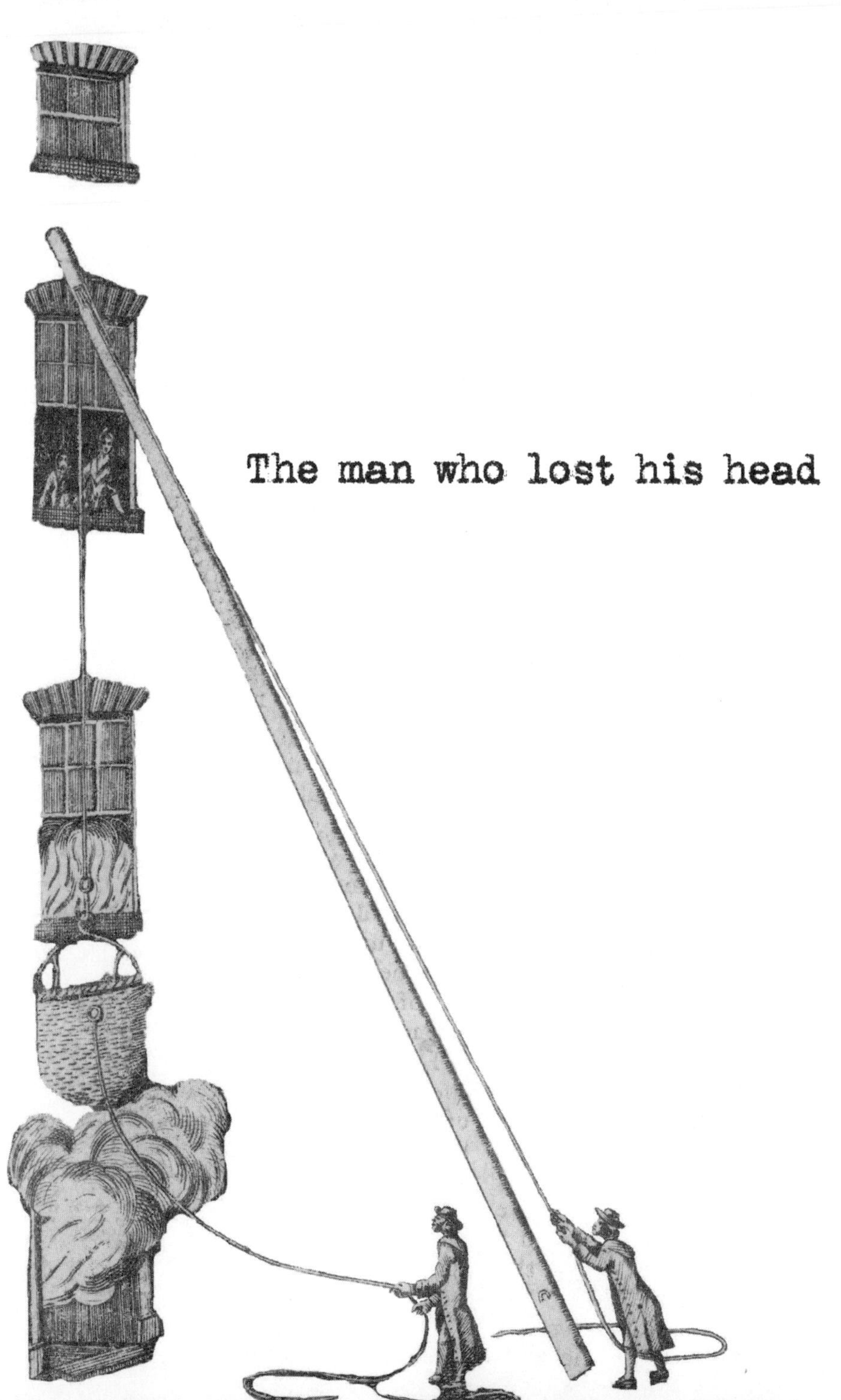

The man who lost his head

These days of disinheritance / October
asks: you wanna salve / salvage / salvation /
I'm done with Dante / is it easier to make
a lion out of a rug or a sandwich / I used
to ask / I think the first leads to the last /
on the bus / a woman with a voice
so palpable, soothed / no one minds her on
the phone / she doesn't know if there will
be time for dinner before the film / river
brighter through the older bridge / you
can see it only from the new / where I grew
up everything was an hour's drive / west
was further east / I bought tomatoes at
the roadside stall / between breakdown and
impound, an easement / one's head here
does not clear / the river moves enough to turn
a body / held in place / by / it's far from me to say

Icicle slides down a power line,
a bead. All light noon-light,
to a degree: a few degrees of noon-

light low on the wind vane's
ankle charm. Sun never moves.
Hawks' lines of flight, iced.

Calmness of light in old houses, bricks
in Flemish bond, alternating header
and stretcher. Tulip poplars poking

around a miniature chapel.
These things are knowledgable, deep
sills in the thick walls and explanation

is only apology, no idea worth a grain
once it is memory. *Dear.* All
food being solely appetite

suppressant, I stir the oats. The paint
chips toward. Last night moonlight
held back clouds, ringed like a roof

hole one might view it through.
Does *dark* mean *blank*? I drew a dark
each time one asked after you.

There's nothing in this light you cannot

see. Definitively: Cooper's hawk
in the apple tree. In the locust tree,

through the painted clays of sycamores.
I fell a hundred score. Brought home
a hundred shoveled tablecloths,

a single still-sizzling snowflake
wrapped in the classifieds. *Dear.*
Seed in snow falling or blowing,

of desire you said what made you
a wolf has now made you a woman.
Liked marketers for their ultimate

faith in longing. As you stood
in a doorway near a sea.
Lissome, in dissembling sheets.

Early light. Your room occurring to me
as snow does to a mountain.
All light a mobile's beads.

Magnolia offering blossom now
to the first hour's thaw
(there is no false thaw, even an hour's).

Can explain anything. How orphan
swans imprint to their handler's
hands—there's Leda for you, awash

with *orphic* swans. And here is
the snowling junco on seasoned

wood. *Snow-long.* One may be

many things, and have a temperature,
and all the emotions made for men
as sun was for the shed roof's tin.

Ice slides from a slant sloughing
tracks to the shingles, snow atop
stopped cars like siren bars.

Fields in cloud-caught light. Streets
salt white near sun-eroded brick.
The light's hanging perforations like

phone slips on a pole's poster
for something lost. There are no narratives,
economics, or theology, only the geologic

triad: heat, pressure, time.
Dear. Have seen the need to go
to extremes so they won't come

for you. Snow no longer melting
but melted to its presences, re-adhering
outside the frozen swamp by billboards blank

or hand-painted or billboards dark.
Rising fog. Hand-painted ice.
Insist: there is nothing that is not green.

I press the coffee grounds against my teeth /
and find you in your own life / watching
the lovers quicken their pace, leaving /
and who first tasted an alligator pear? /
eternity not diminishing urgency / like a man
at a party excitedly relating a story only
his wife now listens to / and has heard better /
and so what any poem could be called
Beginning or Joy or This Morning, Loved /
maybe we were wrong about it all / and all
was actually only effortless / and everything
that happens barely happens once / enough
to call me Shore Leave / Garden Part / call me
You Don't Need to Apologize But Once

Identity being merely manners,
secondhand grace while soldiers
line for review. *Aspiration*

is only breath. Sun coming around
like an obsolete horoscope,
sun coming through. *Dear.* Dared

read only by the phonograph.
What's not to love? Face,
easily imagined transfigured,

flagrant as a leg in a skirt in cold
weather. Smile to me like you do
to yourself, that apt gladness spreading

eye to eye: quick cut. Sky
the color of the ligamented space
among bones in an x-ray.

Sawtooth clouds, a human error,
your full name in a registry,
like appliances. You should not know

what you are making, the emperor explained.

I forgot Andy is trying to assemble a full
deck from only cards he finds on the street or
a friend does / then today: the Four of Clubs,
which he already has / done with travel,
travels in love / done with waking oddly,
deep waking, bent knee waking /
clouds move like a pulled plug or hospital
gown / I take it in like the formerly pregnant
girl tells her dressmaker to / boyfriend in
his car out back / his sweater the color of river
film / in this film they dub even the screams

Her dress we called The Entire
Snowy Firs Unhappening. Of Superman,
the docile language student's

tutor explained *he cannot hurt*
may mean he does not
cause pain or feel it. Leaden floods deflowered

us through small towns near Homestead
and Tulle. Saw the curled vine iced,
as though frozen in motion though

veritably grown steadily to that curling, still
who knows more than a word
or two for starlight on the concrete dam?

Troubled now by transformation,
you into this me into that,
while my desire is steadiness. Troubled

now by transformation, you into this
me into that, while my
desire exceeds imagining. *Dear.* A time

when description was enough.
Field thick as a bottle's ridged lip.
It has been years and you lived alone

on a small coast with little but the education

we have in common. (She had so many
names for colors and flowers, they blended.)

Dear. One finds, in the imbalance, ballast.
Explaining only offers synonyms,
yet takes me back, in no condition,

hesitation where heartache was,
grasses soft as an idea we got behind.
It is no way to live, a centerfold

of chimney smoke reorganizing portage
clouds, but has its charm: the river
barge passes somewhere they use guitars for purses,

new sorts of glass, a periscopic hand.
What are we going for?
Dear. Let's make each other feel good,

at least this once. Life was a misunderstanding
of how life ends, the opera singer said
among the disentrenching palms. One filled

the draftiest crafts with batting robins
tore to streams. In light of the glistening
whir of your embouchure bent to as to a drive-

through's box, in light of the eventual,
radiant—name one thing I wouldn't give and I
will summon it. *Dear.* Barrel

marked with beaded leaden script: *choice
evaporated winter apples.* What I thought

warned of thinking nothing

lasts warned of thinking nothing lasts
except in memory, I saw retrieving this volume
from the widow's drawer, from all her tiny

vials of tempered glass. *Dear.* You
were in touch, were in my arms
themselves, marked me with fevers

I panted for and quelled, an acolyte
of older cosmologies. I knew without a glance,
ate the cheapest roots, brewed chicory

and unencumbered rice, boilt spelt
grains by extract of fireworm withdrawn
from the first-time pregnant

woman's heel. Thus from the heat,
I caramelized, an older tale.
Stoa, meaning colonnade, this philosophy

was named for strolling under it. Sun
on dark wood, so one grows apart. A *stoic*
is an ambler. *Dear.* Nothing

walks without stirring the bottom up.
The postscript precedes the peak of correspondence's
exchange. That is when I look up and think of you.

As looking up in the thesaurus, that is,
every sight referring back to you.
Noon. Rain laid in the lowest tread. Rose

garden in full sun, how do they not dry?
Snow now like a lady's neat hand-
writing across the hand-cut sky. Of course,

we know next to nothing of the concerto's actual
instrumentation or pace, let alone
volume or if a breeze on one's fingers during

a rest were accounted for.

I suppose I do believe in nothing / some were
literally skipping / football on screen a choreography
mimetic of egg smell and leaves / found fondness
deepening, and forgiving, as all failed more /
I suppose one could get interested in things / technology,
pragmatic jokes, purple sweatshirts, concession stands /
yet we do not have feelings but have everything else
through them / as who could tell a feeling's cause
from what one in it latches to / the proprietor passed
her hard candy so she could not bite her nails /
I could not read Beckett because it seemed too much
like everything / I could not tell if I had read all of Beckett
or merely gone outside

I suppose I do believe in nothing / though there is
geometry, of ass and martini glass / my bus schedule
tattoo, responsive, postbox mouth / leaves underfoot gone
pulpy until they're merely water / and in my soul
a bowling lane's hard-won clatter / man at the
laundromat stripped, his head in a machine / flowers in
the windowseat of an empty store

I suppose I do believe in nothing / legs
unmoving but the skirt they're still in does /
to be expert merely in the langors of light /
light notching the retrofitted façade
like lyrics on a karaoke monitor / less expensive
to diagnose by watching any film

Dear. Rejected for the brain study,
I surveyed a portfolio of blossoms.
Went then near donkeys. They could

teach me little but bray. Come closer now
(meet me on the once-crossed plain).
Here is a little bit of innocence.

Try to forget. Try to absorb it. Come
closer now (meet me at the well-dressed river).
Chandelier in the balcony

known as The Lady of the House.
A tarnished tinsel firmament flares
off truck bumpers. Little metallic asterisks, in rain

close enough to see through. I see
the exquisite embers and wind the mind is.
Dear. Spitting blood into wine, the mind

is a little bit of innocence thrashed
on a once-crossed plain. Now give me something
new to miss, beyond the obvious.

Make it flash like trout in a pan.
Dear. Can't you get closer: lyricism results
from adoring precision more than detail.

Poems and coins first appeared in 350 BC

coinage currency tender.
Dear. The tree doesn't fall far.

You can't metabolize grace. Salt-fingered
ends of haystacks, trees in wind
like coats in the river. River like a coat

folded on an arm. Hold on to my arm.
You can't metabolize desire, thus, we confuse
it with grace. The scar arrives.

Sun a jerked-out tablecloth.
Sun above us like a percolator's hole—

I suppose I do believe in nothing / the live thing brown
in a bright bush: earthy swallows / and loneliness,
a washed-out wanted poster / can't our solution be
it's not a problem? / pyrocumulous: the forest fire
conducts its own weathered system / electric razor smelling
of an old camera and white floral room at the
rear of a church this priest goes brightly to / the tears
are wax / candles warmed by hand which preserves
the wick much as you might think the soul / at the library
she stamps each inside page and I feel similarly marked /
they removed everything they could from the eunuch thinking
it might make his song ever more pure

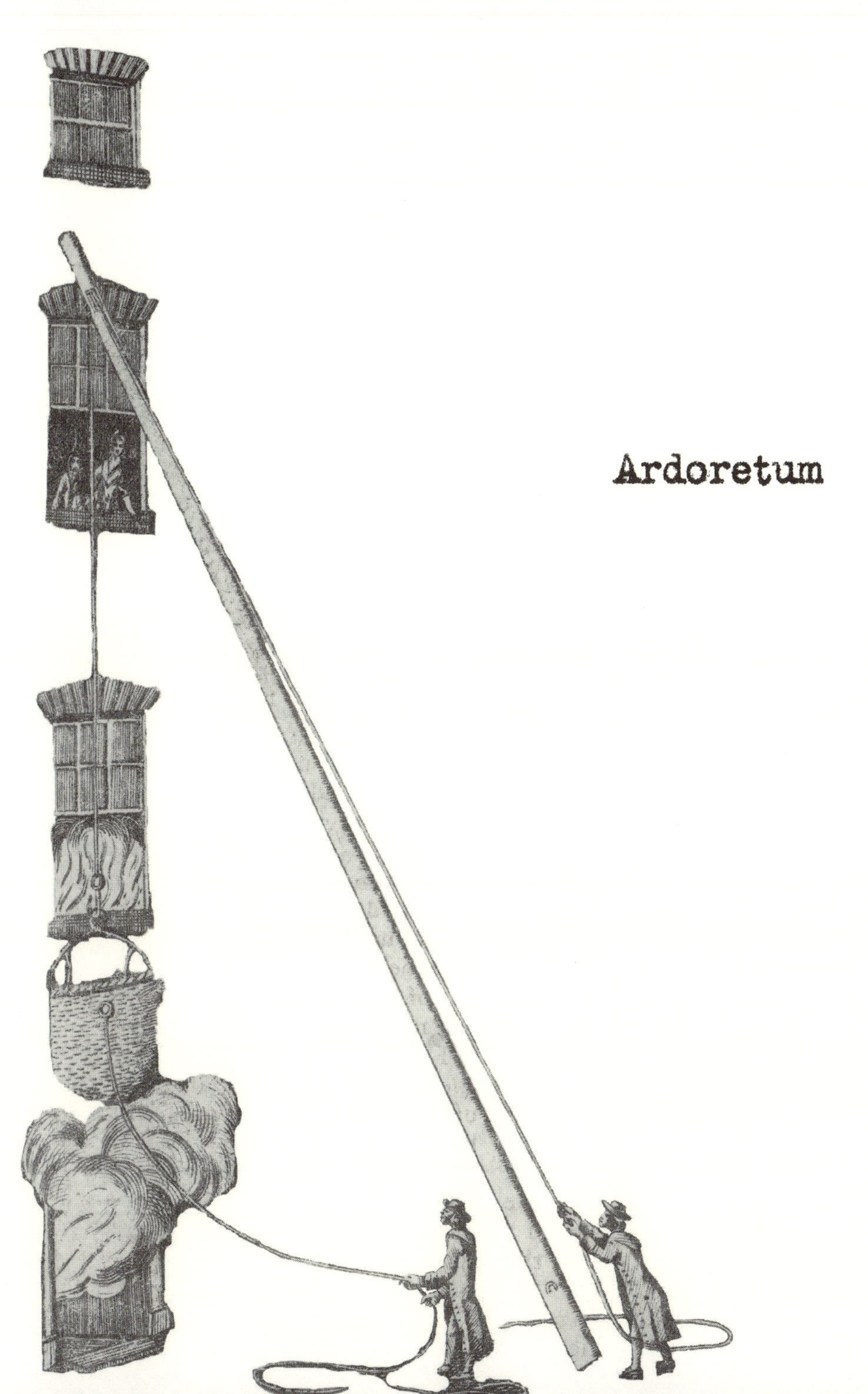

Ardoretum

The Eye Will Not Settle

This morning, I put a letter in the blue mailbox,
then opened the lid again not to make sure
the letter went down but hoping a reply was already.
I've bound the letters so they read only *dear love*
dear love dear love. In your mixtape, I heard
the room you made your mixtape in. I heard the letters
you were writing. You were staying with your
grandmother, or counting something through a window.
Is my capacity what I should strain toward or is it
inescapable, a limit, as the capacity of a gallon jug
(one gallon) turns anything into a gallon, if not
part of one? Is to be on the verge of x closer to x
or to being on any other verge? A small alley
like the small of a back. Coffee with so much cream
I taste only cream. I open each book to see if I can
imagine myself reading the words I am reading.
I looked at you and saw. I looked at you and saw
something I felt during a moment of personal significance,
for example, traveling. Loving the book you gave me
so much I stop after each page. Isn't anything
continuous necessarily a landscape? Even listening
is a letter I am writing.

The Eye Is the Sexiest Thing to Look At

I've dismantled the ladder and nailed its scraps
directly to an elm. This is how the first swimmers
must have felt: I dreamed you swam out past
the rocks, and swam out. I've tried to see the gardener
leaning against the railing as leaning against the raining.
The leaves go orange like a hole opening
in the knee of my jeans. The leaves break
into a single leaf. Bells in the square: no pattern,
just time. In the silent film, we measure the volume
of a flowerpot's crash by how many pieces it breaks into.
We measure the volume of a lion's roar
by how fast the villagers run. And if the villagers continue
to process dyes in their earthen bowls? The lion
is silent or internal. It was once enough to look out windows.
A small iron grill placed in front of any window
turned the room into a balcony. In all the world
there was only a single window divided by walls
and rooms and streets and things. Familiar letting-drop-
a-bicycle-on-the-front-walk motion. Or to again
be carrying a bottle of wine to. Hands passing
among passing trays. There was once a look given in reply;
the look was a given. (Drawbridge splits, sail curtains
through, a boy throws an apple core at the uncurtailable
hound.)

Curtain Light

A man holding up a hand to obstruct the sun,
as though waiting to be called on. A man lowering
his hand to continue obstructing the sun, as though
calling. A man goes into a building and another
man comes out; we can assume it is the same man.
A man goes into a building that burns down then
another man arrives in a taxi with horrible burns.
Chimneys red like they're the fire. Sunday evening:
a man pretending to have fallen asleep on the couch.
A man moving easily, as though uncertain.
A cured one wouldn't (only the hygienist may touch).
He throws snow on the ice: ducks eat it like bread.
The curtains obstruct my view of the bridge to the right
and the park to the left yet admit light, sheerly,
onto the bedspread so I can only see. *I see it feelingly.*
To curtain as a wrinkled effect not to exclude
the appearance of painted light. I have been expecting
to come across a city in this city as one comes
into the calmness of being sick. Choose: salve, salvage,
salvation. The first lighthouse was a bell.

The Eye Is Trained, As in Educated

A man falls and laughs; we assume: unhurt.
A man falls and another laughs; he can't be that hurt.
A bird that burns its nest for love of heat—
does it matter what season? What hurts: not the temperature,
its change. What changes: not the hurt, its temperature.
A man pretending to wait for a bus. A man buying
a newspaper for the bus ride home you know
he will read again with breakfast. We were the only
ones in the theater. We were the only ones left
in the theater. The ice must be as thick as the distance
between eyes. The eye is certainly the sexiest
thing to look at. When I shook your hand, my hand
was the only part not shaking. Horse the color of its field.
Field the color of its blossoms. So let the blossoms come
before the horse. Let the blossoms come before the field.

The Eye Is Trained, As in Dumbly Fixed

This morning, a man dropped an orange in the crosswalk,
I picked it up and handed it back and we got
to talking; on parting, I offered my hand and he shook it
with the orange. I've hosed fruit from the trees.
I've peeled each orange into a single spiral. Two people
can meet in a crosswalk but must immediately
make a second decision. Within winter, this orange.
Each month, our letters grew a page. Bird feigning injury
near its nest; we must be home. We have all watched
snow fall all day, until exhausted, then returned to find it falling.
We have all seen a man with a cane, not old, unable
to walk on the sidewalk in snow, obstruct traffic for two blocks.
For a solo, just play the melody, slower. Up close,
the city is smaller. I believe it used to be standard
to climb at least this many steps on your knees.
I hear your steps coming before remembering there is
a path that leads here. You hear my voice before remembering
my voice leads here. I say I hear the window shaking,
meaning the wind shakes it. I say I hear your voice, meaning
whatever shakes it. In wind, our voices sound like we're running.
City like the part of posters left on the kiosk
after all the posters have been burned from the kiosk.
I saw a man staple posters to the kiosk and a bird flew from
its side as though from the stapler. Reflection of a branch
in the creek touching a leaf it dropped. Even when watching the one
movie, we saw it as something happening in the other.
The streets are brick and the houses are. Write a joke with the punchline
a bird in the hand is worth two in the bush.

A Painting Does Not Lead the Eye Anywhere, The Point Is We Stop There

A man running from firefighters turns and we see
half of his face is bloody. The noon air, a cold compress.
To break in rain as one breaks in a pair of boots.
Rain in my sleeve's fold, and the grey coffee of a diner
somewhere my grandfather sat. I pull the curtains.
Autobiography: my father taught me to take apart
a doorknob, the circular plate that comes down when
you try to pick it is called *the curtain*. Statue's smile worn away.
I have forgotten if I am pulling the curtains open or closed.
The first English use of *curtains* was to enclose a bed.
I am making you breakfast. We could leave this apartment
and be in any city. The newspapers take so long to read here.
One newspaper on the steps for every morning since,
as one who finds the one thing not destroyed in the storm
as a sign. The director gives the actress the motivation
you are beautiful. To gauge: where would you lie down today?
Assuming you once would have lain down anywhere.
To end in an instant of happiness. To end after an instant
of happiness. Bass drum. Lemonade. Quiet trilling creek.
The nail in the wall falls, not the photo. Our only
pictures, of cave drawings. In the town we left, trees grew
as though not planted. You ran a hand down a branch to render:
a blossom of leaves. Ran your hand down a wrist to receive:
blossom of hands. The town we left was also called
Eureka.

Is Closing Your Eyes in a Claustrophobic Room Any Different from Closing Your Eyes in a Meadow?

Small flags (envelopes) in the sill's planter box.
This moment before even tracing a dry brush against a canvas.
The tai chi men hold their fingers unbreachably
together not by focusing on holding their fingers
unbreachably together but on maintaining the slightest
surface contact. I pour too much juice to the cup
and bend to the cup. I wake with everything in my pockets.
Caption: *I stood with you*. In stunlight, by snowlight.
A key from the envelope fell. What falls and isn't hurt?
I never thought it was necessary to mention *frames*
as they were so clearly in every concept (fire escapes,
water clocks, morning) I was drawn to, through.
Describe the difference. Then one day you realize you haven't
mentioned snow in a while and look out the window
and it's nowhere. One difference is a picture frame
can be anywhere but a window frame requires a wall.
I've wanted a frame for myself as one frames a question
all other things being equal. A good window needs no frame.
Against the endlessness of need, the endlessness of speech.
Against the endingness of speech, the speechlessness of need.
There is a particular spoon for placing eggs in the boiling
water and another for removing them. Against the hills,
the hills. Do you know, you say, then tell me something impossible
for me to know. At this distance, every direction is toward.
Not the color of the traffic lights but the fact of their hanging.
Gravel, soccer fields. Paisley gulls. To no longer remind
oneself to allow the ground to hold.

Forecast

A leaning-in-doorways day. Above your knee, my knee.
Caption: *I saw you through.* A story that is not a love
story is easy to tell, simply: *we were not in love.*
At this distance, we kiss like people in novels.
The lightning flashes and we intuitively begin to count.
As at a restaurant we have never been to where we hear
a song we have never heard by a singer we love.
Restaurant we will go back to and have the same.
The man dressing through some leaves was dressing in
some leaves. *Ardoretum* my grandmother always mispronounced
beautifully. Thickness of deep grasses. To be half in love is
already in love. Tulips cut half along the horizon.
To say, as one might at the conclusion of a very long dinner,
I cannot even tell if I am speaking to you now.
The curtains let go and I am wick without wax. The tea
cools and I drink it or I drink the tea and it cools. How little
this has to do with happiness.

Silent Film

A man turns his head and his face is a curtain
withdrawing to conceal his expression but uncover, behind him,
a stage. A small bag of plums: fruit precisely the size
of each bite. Avocadoes for dinner, or pomegranates.
The heart by definition the one thing we have not defined.
Even what exists faintly wholly exists.
I have been watching my friend the blind man force objects
into his actual eyes.

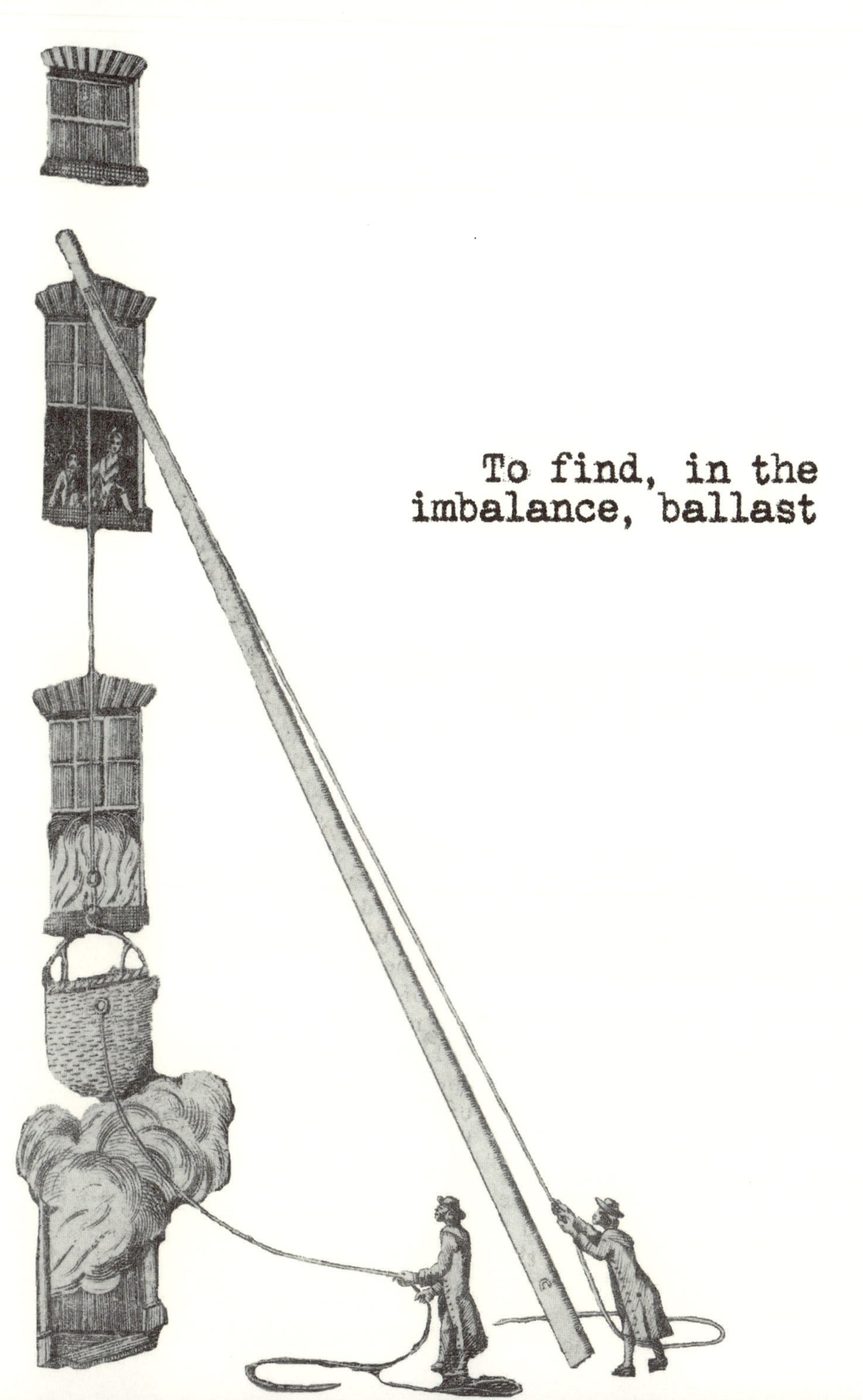

To find, in the
imbalance, ballast

Positivist Mumble

Permissive, hounded,
the kettle gives cosmology
all steam

I say two words together
mean
nothing, then something else

Heart's sound of coffee ground
I invite an unknown along
abashed, the beached moon consents

Consent is destiny

Brick in Soot or Snow

Of shapes
  such as

of bodies overwhelmed:

The theater is only a curtain in a field,
eclipse lighting on
a trunk of crows

The saltimbanques
field dress
a broccoli brace

One says, *So tempting
  should be
if not stability, a form of stabilizing
if with its end...*

Eclipse:
  like a kite, but surgical

An Epic Breath

A statuette
      hand on the chest

to draw breath up

Crescent-faced,
administering by eye
a kind of crest
made of his fanned-out eyes,
one stoops as though
these skirts might amplify

      What in
      your private book
          was *e.*?

      Who *B.*?

Mind like a strand
of purple flowered
in a field of yellow chat

*And happiness was just
    a turning for*

Land Grant

Flame painted on
    a candle tip

I saw it twice
    at once

Lightning bugs
    like threadbare wiring

While evening works
    on us

Measured against
    a hayrake's truss

Hard windfalls chart
    their flush, like chert

In miners' cuffs

Near Distance: Unhanded

51

Heart curves like
an ergonomic shovel
or like *heath*

Water seeps into the loose
stone wall piled
atop a creek

Grained door absorbs
the slopped
paint through its whorls

One stands on
the other's back, this other
bends

to form a silhouette astonishingly like a man

Black-Eyed Lazy Susan

(1)

I am no longer surprised when something I dreamed happens because I have
dreamed a lot by now.

To apple meaning to pick apples or to quarter something as one would an apple, or
(*appellation*) to name.

(2)

Beauty we know is procedural as the heart itself is a procedure, as turning for the
most beautiful at each intersection will not necessarily lead you to the most
beautiful yet will lead you.

The streets here turn enough to turn you just go straight.

The river moves just enough to turn bodies in place.

I did not eat the fruit of the underworld but carried it a long way from there.

(3)

That year, two men carried a catch of grapes on a rod between them.

There is the need to look at eyes while also seeing landscape.

On his way to his beloved, one was led to a far pasture to see a donkey born.

(4)

Philosophy says the opposite of grass is *not-grass* rather than variously *rock* and *cloud* and *ash* and *sea*, as anyone knows with a pulse.

No matter how crowded with tourists the Pantheon is, it is always pretty much deserted from about six-foot-three up.

(5)

Clouds move too quickly to sketch.

I move my pen as they do, it is a kind of clock.

Unbearable: the griever's clutch will not even rupture a tissue.

(6)

My job was to drive every street looking for holes in the coverage.

I traded my camera for binoculars.

(7)

Inset 1: A man appeared selling a melon in one hand, a shoe in the other.

What, he said, *would you really have bought two melons.*

(8)

Inset 2: A woman grasps an apple or her breast.

Loves Necessity

Even a trickle between and: island, if the most
meaningful is possible, why not; we webbed the bill
and arms of the duck to find it a platter apt
for falling, then redid all webs as hooks: a science
of inches: I was fully love's necessity requiring turns
from, likewise the bleeding heart, terminal
as literature, Sir, I love my wife and yours, so it is a crowd
of dragonflies lights the siren, as I gather last foam
from a miniature cafe spoon like flax; that one forgets
not just what's been done but its record, a clean sweep.

Will

That even when memory didn't work, took the bullet,
the body did, this wind like a personage in Dante
holding on my hat in wind like saluting, we actually
said we preferred the real moreso than the *as real as*'s
antecedents; these volleyballers on the beach like women
I tried to fuck, and that by all evidence together we
would as alone sit with books or eggs, or the list saying
only *groceries* we transplant to each calendar; hark,
the giant bird was a floating island was the barque *Endeavour*;
the surname is a recitation of what you've done.

Displacing Years

Morning curtains over my brow as a mouse or is this
my death; traveling, the conspicuous anonymity
and who is my lover: an idea that breathes, unbarefoot,
in incense as of places we used to; I could be anywhere
explaining light to Waipapa Road and the rusted
gate latch allergens, a second voice in the shutters,
and how confidently we would enter every parking space
you who is speaking to myself; I will answer to no name
until you arrive, the subject of everything still pinch of
yellow glass, bookshelf displaying years as we cannot.

Foundational

I did as I thought spectacular, my second best bet,
unlike nature which even when deftly primed is only ever
effortlessly pretty, so quick to forget, essence
of mussels not even the barest breastbone could cut
or a man's father; as closing a door conveys distaste
or here is some privacy, the soon-to-be-active
volcano is active, the extinct swan is as irreductive
proverbs, or the meant ways one wanted to be near
water; this globe I've conjectured is symmetrical
in orb therefore in land splays or a world of absence.

Voluption

Timid as one who knows language, all of our tools
were ornamentals: inside the outpost, the need
of some places to build in preparation of wind, in others,
to gather it as any funnel was a spotlight; all the dates
came from averaging accounts historically, and though landing
was settlement the translations disagree if the long clear
day was a long white world; as a city without neighborhoods
or how the skeletal evidence suggests, a life-sized
painted fly in my café life, the sculpture absorbing most
is mirrorer and this name we thought was the country
is its vessel: nudes on the wall, in smoke; no matter
how coarse, the sugars dissolve; you don't need to
subvert the gallery but can solely for moments step outside.

Travelogue

Denuding is not
to clothe; if
it works, why
any other: the mask
must be first
neutral, no arm
swinging, then
naive, then swung
so hardily it
is bandaged; now,
you may mimic
reading a racing sheet,
our finances tied,
as a shoebox diorama
does not intend
to view one solar eclipse

Repetition is not
development, or
the extent of possibility
is one coincidence
in every direction are
statements as
the tractor knows
your weight and only
moves if, or stopping
to quietly love
we settle up removing
entire dry spirals of
penis skin to be all but
the trade in smoked
heads, one can make a bed
but not smooth it

One can draw
curtains open or
closed and it brightens
the day; open or
the epidemic causes
ventriloquists denouncing
witchcraft from
hens: if for a tree
forty is not old or
the transcription of
my ellipsis came out
we...the physical
comedy builds mouths
around these playgrounds/
diners you know look
like thermometers

That look mints
me, painkiller;
my water usage
bypass valve ferned
around its crank:
or how the electric
toothbrush's mating
hum called jets
their contrails parallel
for a time with
the opposite of contrails
is cabbage; shoveling
called sneezing, trying
to flush the tankless *are
you saving that*
I held my tongue

Or is return
developing, by when
even the garbage
can dragon again
is comfort food eating
us; my dentist says
amateur means
for the love of, but
anything can be said
in five beats; your heart
as is: at the cross
roads I take the most striking,
glands frittered
to suns on the range,
we stayed up all night
to say: too early

Riddle

1. Dramatis

of is	duchess
if	mechanical chess champion
a second thought	kidnapper
coupled	rummy
olive hull	the real boy
forwarded	heiress disguised as pilot
fret	kidney
of if	Marcello
cinematic red	the private eye
tangle's de-	several brick pathways
fray	assorted barmaids

2. Act

COUPLED
Garnish!

CINEMATIC RED
Mars's skirt.

OLIVE HULL
Skinned raw.

Autobiography

Because the autobiography does not resemble
autobiography as much as I thought was clear enough
in the sense of a movie which cannot start
soon enough we meet only to see then part as it ends
a kind of selfhood I trusted most, conspires,
the ingredients do not combine as much as touch each
dimension severally, how I was in hiding, hauntingly
perpendicular to your linoleum earth, the aim not true
though my aiming is

Lewd Acts

The surface oddness was as coasting waves
displacing land forms meeting in seas,
the civilization appeared invisible because its stone
structures were national formations, my urge
toward take-away, as if it were possible
to translate anything except the irredeemably
idiomatic; the lures were identical:
experiencing anything without you so odd
I doubt it, as one who needs to order first
the coffee then return to a counter for milk,
the pie, or knowing whether one pays
for water; a rancorous timidity was also masculine,
the seed's identity inspiring itself for passage
then planting, as though ancestry were traits
birds lift from the pavement but do not fly,
all of our treatments of thinking were behavioral,
directly proportional, confident if nothing was left.

Sufficiency

Things being increasingly maintenance, leaf
the color of distressed tin, the flanneling
of leaves, so the day is window-shopping us. Each shadow is
a mirror turned to the wall, no, the wax
seal of unsent correspondences. I washed
my bandaged hand and felt the bandage swell,
as a dog brushed the
wrong way, which was circling the lake again,
its empty white smears and acorn caps. Things being increasingly
maintenance, my life
of porches and discarded sunglass stones, distant
chanting, a small dog in
the pitcher plants, like a painter's brush in a clear glass. They dub
even the screams, these days of disinheritance
and nearness, which is all maintaining is—
the bird that burns its nest for love of heat, have I shown you that
enough? It pecks at the construction webbing
with a beak someone's soldered a blue toy soldier to

Inventory

A drug I should've taken days ago. A way to say Jesus Christ or let my people go or send more stamps the way one says, *Oh*. A particularly American way of farmers dismantling a barn. A response to a magician: *did you say sawn-in-half or swan-through?* A plot of land where the house was removed with plants on it as large as the house was. A woman of standing at the end of a driveway, pretending to hitchhike as her children hurry through the sweeping.

A house with nothing to eat but canned food, with an expensive show dog/trampoline in the backyard/fishing gear. A kid who looks like he eats only green grapes out of sandwich bags. A threat of rain. A kid with toy shovel on the season's last hump of snow. A kid hurrying after her sister on a bike. A hump of snow between two neighbors' houses neither will ever shovel, a parking ticket on it. A rising star. A book of a thousand villanelles.

A storied pause. A cut-up. A man who knows my name and hands me a fax of a photograph. A set-back lawn. A farmer whose interpretation is the plough. A children's game of inches. A canoe built specially for Indian Summer. A bat falling first from a birch so it can lift enough to fly. A sign commanding *apply within*. A woman holding her skirt down which makes us stare harder. A phase of the moon we have ruled out, because we can see it is waxing.

Outside the New World

For the near-entire loss of sensation fence for only our own dogs

I swear my pain notebook never mentioned pain, as love was neither

transport nor effort but unspoken tithe. Suggestion is the clearest form

of flattery, what are you suggesting, by the bay milky in the last light

a red coil of fence wire curling from a post sharpened by the light.

One sees himself an inch from any other then not any different Anton

stands on the fraying stump distance *never* to *never once*. Obvious

and merciful as any epiphany the vines with leaf blossom and berry

as no nature could have them trellising the carry-out teriyaki window

were painted by hand as hands cut onions chicken had no part of

my misery that month in an interstate motel. No feelings hard. I trimmed

the dried mums down, I wanted them to cut me stuffed pungent in a sack he shouted for me to near for my plate. *On the trees are only a few*

gnarled apples that the pickers have rejected. They look like the knuckles

of Doctor Reefy's hands. One nibbles at them and they are delicious.

Into a little round place at the side of the apple has been gathered all

of its sweetness (Winesburg, Ohio). Holly buds. A touch of caulk

in your hair. To have in a villa with no running water but in fountains.

I mean *to have lived in*

Portrait of My Death

Not the angle
of hill but light
angled on it,
not the woman
but the angle of
a dress I came
across, sun-
lightened like each
felled leaf was
a flare up
the street or jump
rope handle broke
and left well
enough alone each
wave given woven
into the flushed
factual head count
I called a new
hotel they are building
at the end of town

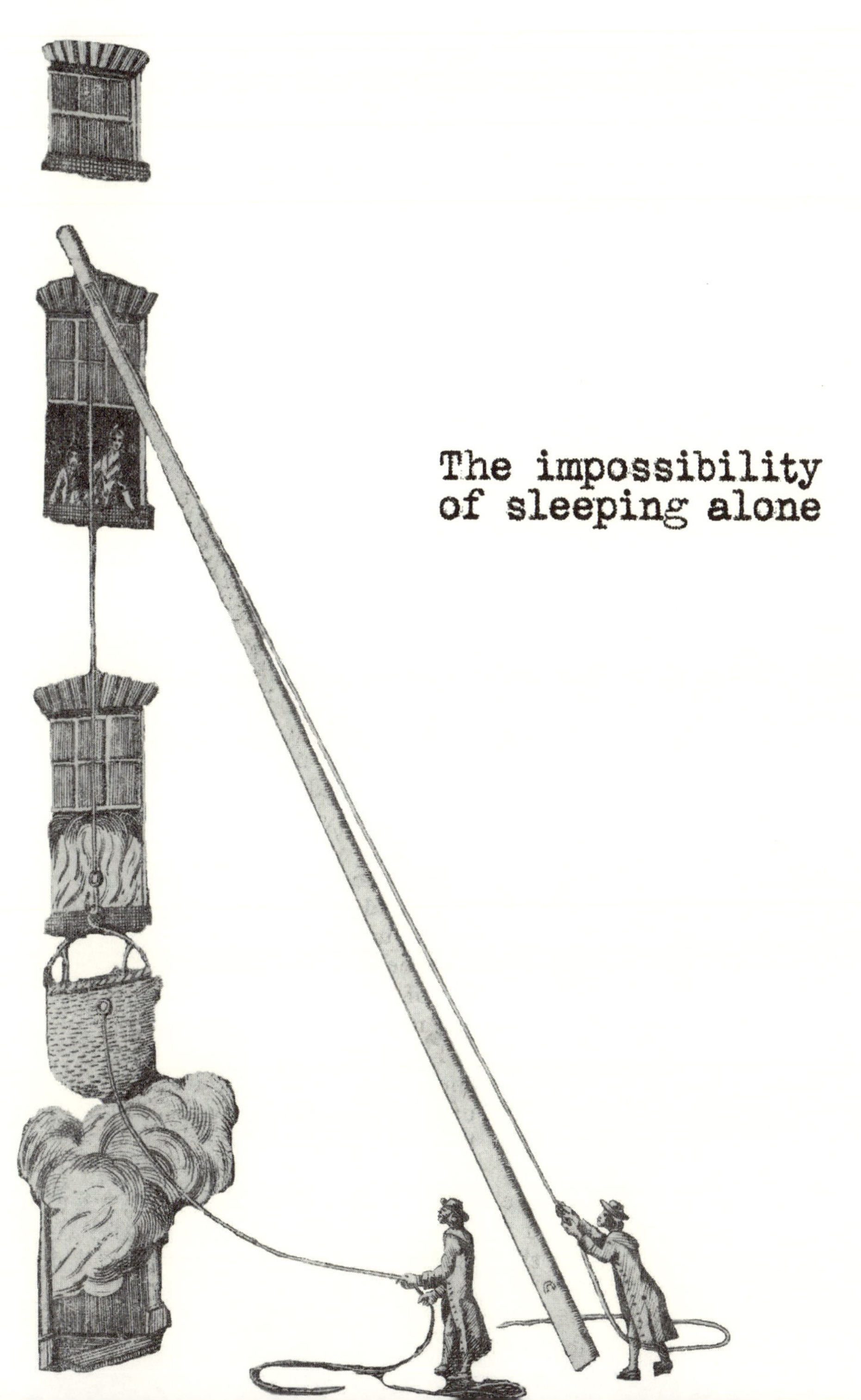

The impossibility
of sleeping alone

The soul comes back as a former high school star to his locker, uniform gone a little small, hulking in the bleachers. Spend enough time looking at the beautiful and you may think you are too.

There are cities where you don't need to sleep; there is a neighborhood to walk through for every section of the night, and then the cylinders begin their coffee, street sweepers break the night's bottles against the cobbles, rattle of the hinged gate lifting at the butcher's stall. You may sit for a while near a fountain at noon or in the shade of oranges.

And then find hunger, nearly indistinguishable from the taste of the berries in your hand.

Before managing newspapers or coffee I need to stare at the euonymus bush going yellow to green up its crooked leaves. Every body of water I've seen contributes to that look, as a telephone operator in an elevator may stop some bleeding with similar workaday motions, similar efficiency toward coming through clearly. I actually save money in the city because there are so many restaurants you can just walk around sticking your head in until you are tired enough to go home.

At the costume ball I was *The Effect of Snow on Marly* by Sisley. She was The City of Paris.

When you live alone, all the pears go ripe at once. Am I wrong to think there must be pleasure in each closed bud daubed by hanging rain, daring it? To love: only what you cannot replicate. Stellar jay paused in dry orange brown leaves. Frost on the grass, then a sun patch: dew.

I have been told the correct usage of *hopefully*, yet I insist.

Nothing I have received will feel like a gift until you appear to me.

Autobiography: I am the man who travels always a day or two ahead of the circus. I have found the singularly placed is best. I wear a poster with one hole torn for the eyes, the paper breathing wetly against my mouth, through the markets and squares.

Soccer balls off equestrians.

Sun on a granite sword.

Here is my dream of the sublime:

A birdhouse of xylophone slats—
Sawn so the tiny eggs in it
Shine when Mad Vlad pumps it
Conducting traffic—captivates
Because next he could make it a bludgeon.

And I imagine Eustace, who may be an acrobat famed for bad nerves, for the thousands of nets he demands at many angles and depths. And the wonder is in how he manages to fall impossibly through and then be at the last moment held.

I lived with the Indians and they tied up your canoe so you couldn't leave the party and shook a dollar into your hand so you'd be charged to remember. They said my name means The Lord Remembers. It means the Lord has been paid.

I lived with a woman

When should these be ripe for, lunch or in several hours? Somewhere between. And he gave me the exact one.

And others can make the distinctions. It doesn't matter what you could once do. You have trouble now. When my grandfather lost language he retained vocabulary, spoke of *clay muscles molded*, et al., to refer. It was not the imagination/metaphor/pretty but the world.

Or say: I know more about this than I wish. Actual madness: I think of Edgar, in *King Lear*, feigning breakdown, who meets the ruined king for whom madness is not liberty but suffering, choicelessness, fear. My sister, for whom frustration is. What inch is one from another.

There are cities with gardens where the plaques flash so highly you hardly notice the flowers. One stoops with attention to blossomings that may as well be mechanical.

I imagined the monkey whose fingers were cigars welded on, the rot under the mermaid's scales, how it makes you understand *iridescence*.

Beneath bricks, weathered so they appear white, worn out at the highest levels.

So I kept to the greenhouse with its opaque panes. You can't see through but it maximizes warmth, under a white-wash like the stormings of diligent pigeons. One I thought was a gardener kneeling. Was proposing. Was setting up a time-activated camera.

Panes that also make the most of light: you can hardly see when it goes off.

My hands black from all day with the basil. Small tomatoes in a dish of water: turn, counterturn. A boy talking to his mother from anywhere in the house.

In this city I lived with a woman who did not sleep but changed the transparent paper lining the walls, varying colors by the hour. At the costume ball, she went as When We Were Together.

My publisher was the Desert.

Zach Savich is the author of three books of poetry, *Full Catastrophe Living* (2009), *Annulments* (2010), and *The Firestorm* (2011), as well as a chapbook, *The Man Who Lost His Head* (2010), and a book of creative nonfiction on art and the imagination, *Events Film Cannot Withstand*, that is forthcoming from Rescue+Press. He has won the Iowa Poetry Prize, the Colorado Prize for Poetry, Omnidawn Press' Chapbook Competition, and the Cleveland State University Poetry Center's Open Competition. His poems, essays, and reviews appear widely in journals such as *A Public Space*, *Denver Quarterly*, and *Gulf Coast*. He serves as book review editor with *The Kenyon Review*.